Your Feelings and

What God

Says About Them

D1607683

Inspired by God
Written by Julie Chapus

Your Feelings and What God Says About Them
Author: Julie Chapus

PUBLISHED BY:
Five Stones Publishing
A DIVISION OF:
The International Localization Network
randy2905@gmail.com
ILNcenter.com

All scripture was taken from the Zondervan Life Application Study Bible NIV Copyright 1988, 1989, 1990, 1991 by Tyndale House publishers, Inc Wheaton, IL 60189

Service on Jealousy and Depression by Pastor Joshua Finley, Elim Gospel Church, Lima, NY

Christ for Kids
Ministries

To my daughter given to me from the Lord. May He always be with you, always guide you, and always protect you. He loves you with a great love that never ends and nothing will ever be able to take His love from you.

Table of Contents

Special Thanks

To my Father in heaven, thank You so much for filling me with Your Spirit and for helping me along the path You have chosen for me. This book and the knowledge that fills the pages are Yours alone. Thank you so much for sharing Your wisdom with me and all who read this. I am humbled and filled with gratitude and awe over all You have done. Thank You so much Father. I love You. Amen.

My husband, my partner and friend for life. You have supported me in doing things I had never dreamed possible. Your support and love through the years have made it possible for me to serve God in everything He has called me to do. I love you and I can't wait to see what God has in store for us next. The Good Lord could not have given me a better husband.

My mentor Rev. B.R. Van Dame Weirich. Thank you so much for pouring all of your time and energy into me for so many years. You have brought me up in the Lord and trained me in all of His ways. Your support through the years has meant more to me than you will ever know. My walk with God is all because you took the time to care and to pour His love into the future generations. Words cannot adequately express my deepest gratitude and love. May I pass the torch on as you have done.

Thank you as well to my family, parents, and friends who have encouraged me to follow God, and to Pastor Josh at Elim Gospel Church.

Thank you to Wegmans Supermarkets for helping give me a great start in life with your scholarship program.

Thank you to 5 Stones Publishing. May this book help many children and their families.

Mandy and Jen, thank you for all the prayers and encouragement through the years. I'm so glad God has caused our paths to cross.

A Note to Parents

This book came about after my then-nine-year-old daughter started sharing with me her struggle with bad thoughts. After listening to her, I knew that God wanted me to help her and show her what He has done for me, so she would understand how God can help her, too.

I also knew that the best way I could do this would be to write down many of the things God has been teaching me, in language that a child could understand. Once I started writing, I soon realized that these lessons weren't meant just for me, but for all of God's children who are struggling with the many sorts of problems that we all face in our lives. So what started as a conversation with my daughter eventually turned into this book.

This book contains a list of feelings, emotions and issues that children and teens may be struggling with, along with relevant passages from the Bible that address those issues.

1. It is intended to help young people learn God's ways of dealing with their problems.

2. Scriptural verses are mostly paraphrased in this book and reference numbers are included throughout.

My prayer is that this book will help your child learn how to handle problems, and to realize how much he or she is loved—truly loved—by God.

How to Use This Book

Each of us has had to deal with bad feelings from time to time. Sadness, anger, jealousy—the list goes on and on.

But God does not want our lives to be filled with problems and bad feelings. God loves us and He wants us to have good feelings in our minds and in our hearts. He does not want us to struggle. He wants to help each and every one of us. (Philippians 4:6-9)

In order to help us find those good feelings, God has given us instructions on how to deal with any problem we may be having. When we deal with our problems God's way, a great feeling enters our hearts. Jesus calls this feeling *peace*. God wants us to have peace in our minds and hearts all the time, instead of feeling bad.

This book collects much of what God says about our problems and how we should handle them. It also contains prayers that you may want to say to God. It will be most helpful if you read the prayers in the *"Say these out loud"* sections every day, out loud. Don't just do this once—keep on doing it every day until you start to feel better.

If you follow God's Word, and His ways, one day you will wake up and realize that the problems you have been struggling with are no longer bothering you. You will actually have peace. It's really amazing. Always remember, God loves you very much, child. Just ask and it will be given to you. This is God's promise to you and to everyone. (Matt 7:7)

If you would like to experience peace, read this book all the way through. Since so many problems we face can lead to other problems, you may find it helpful to read the entire book first. Then, if you are still having problems in a certain area, go back to that section of the book. (You'll find a list of the problems discussed in this book in the Table of Contents.)

Look up the thoughts, feelings or emotions you are struggling with, and turn to that page. You will see a description of the problem and a set of instructions on how to handle that particular problem in God's way.

I pray that this book will help you to have that great feeling of peace in your heart and in your mind and that you will truly understand how much God loves you. Amen.

Anger

"Help me! I feel so angry!"

Just about everybody feels that way sometimes. Having angry feelings can really make you feel bad inside, and if you don't know how to manage your anger, it can hurt other people too. If you are feeling angry, ask yourself these questions:

1) Why am I angry?

2) Am I angry because I see someone hurting another person, or doing something bad?

3) Do I have a good reason for being angry?

When someone hurts another person, for a bad reason, we sometimes call that injustice. When we see injustices happening, it can make us angry. If you see something happening that is hurting someone, you should ask God to help you know what you can do about it.

The Bible (Mrk 3:5) tells us that one day, Jesus saw a man who had a bad problem with his hand. Even though everyone could see that the man needed help, no one would help him, because it was a special day of the week, called the Sabbath. Those other people believed that there were a lot of things you weren't supposed to do on the Sabbath day—not even to help somebody who clearly needed help! When Jesus looked around and saw that no one was helping the man, he became angry. Jesus did not stay angry, however. Instead, He turned toward the man, and told the man to hold out his damaged hand. When the man did, his hand was healed. So instead of focusing on His anger at those other people for not helping, Jesus focused on what needed to be done to help the man. He felt angry, but his anger led him to fix the problem.

It's OK to be angry when you see something wrong, but you must use your anger properly. Don't let your anger take control of you; instead, let it motivate you to help solve the problem, or, if you can't solve it by yourself, to find someone who can help. (If you are very young, you may want to tell your parents or someone else you feel safe with what you saw or heard that is making you angry.) If you are angry over something bad or wrong that is happening, the following prayer may help.

PRAYER

Dear God, I see something that is making me angry. Please help me be a part of the solution. Lead me to the people who can help, and guide me to do what is right. Amen.

Not all anger is caused by seeing injustice, though. There are lots of things that can cause a person to feel angry. Not all of those reasons are very good reasons, however. For example, sometimes you might feel angry because you didn't get something you wanted, or because things didn't turn out the way you were hoping they would. Maybe you lost at a game that you were playing. Or maybe your parents wouldn't let you stay up as late as you wanted. Or maybe you didn't get the birthday present you were hoping for.

That kind of anger, then, is different from the kind of anger that Jesus felt when he saw that no one would help the man with the injured hand. Jesus was able to use that anger for something good; his anger over what he was seeing made him want to fix the problem, and so he healed the man's hand. But this other kind of anger—anger that's mostly about not getting our way, or not getting what we want, or having our feelings get hurt--usually doesn't lead us to anything good. Instead, it just makes us feel bad inside. That's why, when you're angry, it's important to try to figure out why you are angry. If you find that your anger is mostly about you and your feelings, God can help you. He has given us words that will help give you peace, and take those angry feelings away.

Let's take a look at what God says about anger.

(SAY THESE OUT LOUD)

God shows Mercy. He forgives people. He holds His anger back. Since God made me, I should follow His ways and forgive people too. I will hold my anger back. (Ps 78:38)

God, You have compassion. You are slow to become angry, and You have a lot of love. I can trust You. Help me to have compassion. Don't allow me to hurt people because I am angry. Help me to show love instead. (Ps 86:15)

A fool acts out his anger, but a wise person keeps himself under control. I am not a fool, so I will not act out my anger. I will keep myself under control. (Prv 29:11)

An angry person starts problems with other people. An angry person hurts himself and others. I will listen to God and not hurt myself or other people. I will not stay angry. (Prv 29:22)

Mixing milk makes butter, twisting a nose very hard will make it bleed, and being angry causes fights to start. I do not want to fight, and I certainly don't want a bloody nose, so I will not be angry. (Prv 30:33)

Jesus teaches us to love one another. (Jhn 13:34) If you are feeling angry at someone, apologize to God and pray for the person you are angry at. You will find that praying for the person you are angry at will help you feel better. Do this as many times as you need to. If you said or did something hurtful to someone because of your anger, it is best to apologize to God and then to the person you hurt. This will help you get that good feeling of peace back in your heart. Jesus also tells us that we should pray for those who hurt us, and that we should love our enemies. (Matt 5:44)

The reason why He tells us to pray for the people who hurt us is because they are hurting on the inside too. They don't need someone to be angry at them and hurt them back. They need someone to pray for them, so that they can have peace in their hearts. Once they have peace in their hearts, they won't hurt other people any more. That is why Jesus wants us always to pray for the people who are mean to us and who hurt us. It may not feel very natural, but when you do what God wants you to do, it sure does make you feel good inside. You will get back your feeling of peace, and the more you pray for those other people, the better they will get too.

PRAYER

Dear God, please forgive me for this anger I have. I know that [name of person you are angry at] is your child too, and he/she must really be hurting right now. Please help him/her to heal on the inside, and please give them a sense of peace. I want to have your peace, Jesus. Please bless [name of person you are angry at]. Amen.

Bad Feelings
Toward Other People

Think about all the people that you know. Some of them are your friends. You like your friends, and they like you. But there may be people that you don't like so much. In fact, there may be people that you don't like at all. Sometimes people even talk about hating each other.

God doesn't expect you to be friends with everyone you know. And if someone you know is doing a lot of bad things, it may not be good for you to be around that person.

But when you dislike somebody so much that you start wishing bad things for them, or not caring about them at all, that's a problem.

You see, we are all God's children. He made each and every one of us, and He loves us all the same. The Bible tells us that nobody is God's favorite. (Acts 10:34).

God loves us all equally, and He wants us to love each other. How can you do that if you really just don't like a certain person? Well, God has a lot to tell us about these kinds of feelings.

The first thing we need to do is understand that the person you don't like is still a child of God. So you may not like what they do or what they say or how they act, but you still need to remember that God made that person and He loves them.

So how should we act toward somebody we don't like? What should we say? How do you possibly show love to someone you don't like? Jesus tells us to pray for that person. He also tells us to love, not judge. When we pick out something we don't like about someone, we are judging them. It's best to remember that God loves us all the same, and just because someone is different from you does not make them unlovable to God.

There will be times when you have to see people you don't like, and you may have to be with them or even work or play with them. When that happens, treat them the way you would want to be treated. No matter how somebody feels about you, you certainly wouldn't want them to be mean to you; you'd still want them to be polite and kind. That's how you should treat other people.

Now a problem might come up if you're being nice to somebody on the outside, but thinking bad things about them on the inside. We should always be kind to everyone, but do not be kind to someone's face, and hold bad feelings against them on the inside.

If you do that, you are actually telling a lie—a lie to God. God sees into our hearts, and if you are acting nice to someone, but holding in bad feelings towards them, it's a kind of lie, and God does not want us to lie, to Him or anybody else. (Jhn 8:32)

So what should you do if you simply don't like someone? Should you not be nice to them? No. If there is someone you really just don't like very much, the answer is not to show it, by being mean or disrespectful or unfriendly to that person.

That's not showing love to that person, and God wants us all to love one another, whether we like them or not. Now maybe you're wondering, how can I love somebody if I don't like them? Aren't loving and liking kind of the same thing?

When God tells us to love each other, He means that we should care about each other. We should try to help others who are in trouble and need our help, no matter how we feel about them. And we should never try to hurt anyone, or even wish for something bad to happen to them, whether we like being around them or not.

Jesus told a story once about a man who got badly hurt while he was walking down a road. A lot of people walked by the man, and saw how hurt he was, but they wouldn't stop to help him; they just kept right on walking. Finally one man came along, saw the man lying there hurt, and stopped to help him and get him to a doctor. That man—the man who stopped to help—showed love for the man who was hurt. He didn't know the man who was hurt—he'd never even seen him before—but he knew that the man was a child of God, and that God would want him to help the man. That's a good example of what it means to love others.

So if you know someone that you simply don't like, be honest with God about it, and ask Him to help you to feel love toward that person. The best thing you can ever do about anything is talk to God about it, so tell Him how you feel, and begin to pray for the person you feel that way about. Ask God to bless that person, and ask Him to clean from your heart all the bad feelings and thoughts you are having about that person.

If you are in a situation like that right now, you may find this prayer helpful:

Dear God, please forgive me for having bad feelings and thoughts about [person's name]. Please clean my heart, and bless [person's name].

Continue to pray this way every day, asking God to bless the other person until you are no longer having bad thoughts or feelings about that person. This does not mean that you have to be friends or hang out with the other person. All it means is that your heart must be clean and free of bad thoughts and feelings toward all of God's children. Asking God to bless the other person is actually helpful for you as well as for the other person.

Remember, God sees your heart, and He wants what you do and say to line up with what is in your heart. God wants you to show love to others, and to feel it in your heart too. He never wants us to hate anyone, because He knows how bad it will make you and His other children feel.

(Say these out loud)

Jesus instructed us to love each other. He said, "As I have loved you, so you must love one another. By this everyone will know that you are my disciples, if you love one another."(Jhn 13:34)

I will love others in my words and in my heart by praying for them.

Bullying--Getting Bullied

Allpeople want to be loved and accepted. But sometimes people do not realize that they ARE loved and accepted by God, who loves them more than they can even imagine. Because they do not know how much God loves them, they begin to look for love and acceptance from other people instead.

There's nothing wrong with being loved and accepted by other people, like our friends, parents, and teachers. God wants all of us to love one another. But God's love and acceptance are what really matter. And you don't have to do anything, or act a certain way, to get God to love and accept you. He already loves and accepts you, completely, no matter what.

When you know--truly know--that God loves you, it won't matter when others don't. And if you know, truly know, that God accepts you, it won't matter when others won't. I heard those words from God one morning when I was going through a very bad time in my life. Once I realized how much God really does love me, I realized that I didn't need to try to act cool, or to be friends with all the popular people. God loves me, and I am OK.

Bullies do what they do because they do not know how much God loves them. They think that if they pick on other people, then they will seem tough and cool, and no one will pick on them. The error in this is that God does not want them to bully His other children. When bullies do that, they are actually hurting themselves. If they only realized how much God loves them, they wouldn't need to try to make themselves feel better by picking on people.

If you are being bullied, you must tell your parents, teachers or an adult you trust. You must not hold this in or keep it a secret. It needs to stop, and you must tell someone about it. God also has a very special way to help you too. It is through prayer and speaking God's words out loud.

(SAY THESE OUT LOUD)

God has not given me a spirit of fear. He has given me a spirit of power and love, and a sound mind. (2 Tim 1:7)

He who hates is in darkness. (1 Jhn 2:9)

I will call upon the Lord and be saved from my enemies. (Ps 18:3)

The Lord does not like a heart that plans wicked things to do. (Prv 6:18)

Be strong and of good courage. Fear not and do not be afraid of them, for the Lord God goes with you. He will not fail you or leave you all alone. (Deut 31:6)

Remember, Jesus tells us to pray for our enemies. He said, "Love your enemies and pray for those who persecute (harm)

you, so that you may be children of your Father in heaven."
(Matt 5:44)

So if a bully is picking on you, please tell an adult about it, because you will need an adult to help you. But don't forget to also pray for the bully's heart. Pray that God will help the bully, so that he or she won't hurt you or anyone else or themselves anymore.

Jesus taught us this lesson. When you pray as Jesus tells us to, you are proving yourself to be a child of God, and God will help you.

When you have God on your side, amazing things happen. God will protect you, child. All you need to do is ask Him, and to pray for your enemies. That is God's way.

PRAYER

Dear God, I am being bullied and I really need your help. I pray for [name of bully]'s heart. He/she does not know what he/she is doing. Please forgive this person, God. And please protect me so that I can carry out the good plans you have for my life. Amen.

Bullying—Being a Bully

If you are bullying someone, please stop, for your own sake and theirs. God does not like that, and you are really hurting yourself, far more than you realize. You are actually setting yourself up against God. He loves you, but He cannot tolerate sin, and by being a bully you are sinning against God. That means that you are not living the way that God would like you to. When we don't live according to God's ways, we end up hurting ourselves.

If you wish to have peace in your heart and would like all of the bad feelings you are having to be removed, this prayer may be of help.

PRAYER

Dear God, please forgive me. I have hurt your children. I do not like the way I feel inside. I ask You to enter my heart and teach me Your ways. Please help me to stop hurting others, and show me what I can do to change. I love You, God. I no longer want to be a bully. Amen.

NEXT STEP

Your next step after praying should be to apologize to the people you have hurt. Depending on how far this has gone, you may need to go tell your parents what you have done. This may sound scary and hard to do, but Jesus can help you through it.

Jesus said, "The truth shall set you free." (Jhn 8:32). What does that mean?

Sometimes when we've done something that we know is wrong, we are tempted to lie about it, or try to hide it. It may be because we are afraid of being punished, or maybe just because we're embarrassed or ashamed of what we've done.

But lying or trying to hide the truth is never a good idea. When you lie or hide things, the problem usually ends up becoming worse and worse, because you have to tell even more lies, to cover up your earlier lies. Soon you're sorry you ever lied in the first place, but by then the lie's gotten so big, you're more afraid than ever to tell the truth.

Jesus calls this being a slave. That's right, you actually become a slave to sin (doing these bad things).

Only God can help you break free, and for that to happen, you must do it God's way, and that is by being truthful. Just tell the truth. It may seem hard to do, but once you've told the truth about what you've done and how sorry you are, you will get peace back in your heart and you will no longer be a slave to sin. That's what Jesus meant when he said that the truth will set you free.

The great news, then, is that even if you have been a bully, you can turn things around with God's help. Get serious about needing to change, because the peace that this will give you is a far better feeling inside than you'll have if you hold onto all of the fear that you have right now.

What fear? Fear of getting caught, fear that you will be punished, or that something bad might happen to you if you stop being a bully—maybe fear that no one will like you. The truth is, though, that God loves you. He loves you more than you know, but He does not like it when you act like a bully. God tells us in the Bible that "What you do to the least of these [people around you], you do to me." Think about that for a minute. When you are bullying someone, you are actually bullying God. Now I don't know about you, but that certainly does not give me a warm fuzzy feeling of peace!

You must know that God loves you, child. Say it out loud right now. Just say, "God loves me." Feel it. Once you do that, here are some other things to say out loud. Ask God to move in your heart while you are saying these words.

(SAY THESE OUT LOUD)

Do not judge others, so that you will not be judged. (Matt 7:1-5)

I will do unto others as I would have them do to me. (Matt 7:12)

The Lord is my light and my savior; whom shall I fear? (Ps 27:1)

I will not try to get even with people, or hold a grudge against them, but instead I will love my neighbor as much as I love myself. (Lev 19:18)

Love your enemies and pray for those who hurt you, so that you may be children of your Father in Heaven. (Matt 5:44)

This is such an important subject, let's go over the main points again.

First, please know, dear child, that you are loved, more than you can imagine. God has a good life planned for you, but you must stop hurting others and recognize that you are doing these things because of the hurt that you feel on the inside.

If you pray to God and ask Him for help, and if you stop bullying, God will put peace in your heart, but you cannot do this by yourself. You will need God's help, and God is more than happy to help anyone who asks. "Knock and the door will be opened, seek and you will find, ask and it will be given to you." (Matt 7:7)

Repeat over and over, "God loves me unconditionally." That means God loves you no matter what you have done. He wants you to ask Him for help. He also wants to give you His Holy Spirit, but you must ask for this.

It takes great courage to admit when you have done something wrong, and to change your ways and stop doing bad things. It is worth it, though. The peace and love you will feel on the inside will be far better than any feelings you get when you bully someone.

I sincerely pray that the Lord will guide you into His loving arms. My prayer is that God will truly touch your heart and show you His mighty goodness and His beautiful plan for your life. I also pray that you will find the courage to trust God and change your ways. God bless you, child. Amen.

Compromise–Doing Things
I Know I Should Not Do

When we hear or use the word "compromise," we usually think of it as a good thing. And it often is.

Let's say, for instance, that you and your friend are making plans together. Your friend wants to play basketball, but you'd rather go for a bike ride, so the two of you agree to ride your bikes to the basketball court. That way you're both happy. That's a good compromise. But there's another kind of compromise, that's not so good. What kind of compromise am I talking about?

Let's imagine once again that you're with your friend. This time, though, your friend wants you to help him or her steal something. You know that you shouldn't, of course, but you might be tempted to do it, just so your friend won't get mad at you.

Sometimes we get ourselves into some pretty sticky situations. There are times when we know what we should do, but we want to be liked by people, and we want them to be happy with us, and because of that, we may end up doing things that we know we shouldn't. That's a bad kind of compromise.

When we compromise about what we know is right or wrong, that's called compromising our integrity, or our principles, or our values. That means that instead of sticking to what we know is right, we're giving in and going along with something that we know is wrong.

Doing things that we know are wrong is obviously not a good thing to do, but is it ever OK? We need to turn to God's word and His ways to find out. Let's see what God tells us about compromising.

There once lived a king named Darius. One of the men who worked for him was named Daniel. Darius liked Daniel, because Daniel was an honest man and a hard worker. He always did a good job at any task he was given. Daniel also really loved God. He prayed to God a lot and God helped Daniel do everything well.

Daniel was such a good worker, and the king liked him so much, that some people became jealous of Daniel. They didn't want him around anymore, so they talked Darius into making a new law, which said that no one was allowed to pray to anyone but the king. The law also said that anyone who didn't obey this law would be thrown to a bunch of hungry lions. Yikes!

Now Daniel had a choice to make. He loved God very much and he prayed to God every day, but now the king wanted everyone to pray to him instead of God. Daniel knew that if he refused to pray to the king, he could get eaten up by hungry lions! What would you do in that situation?

Daniel loved God so much, he knew God would help him, but only if Daniel did what was right. Daniel made his decision. He chose to pray to God and not to the king. He did that because Daniel knew God, and he knew that following God is always the right thing to do.

When the king found out that Daniel was not praying to him, but to God instead, he was very upset. He really liked Daniel, and he knew Daniel was a good man, but the law was the law, so he threw Daniel into the hungry lions' den.

I know it seems as if Daniel's decision turned out badly. Daniel chose not to compromise his morals (his sense of right and wrong), so now he was food for the lions. This story certainly does not sound as if it's got a good ending. But let's see what happened next.

Daniel knew that he'd done the right thing by praying only to God, and he knew that God would be with him. Well, he was right about that. God saw what was happening, and He sent an angel into the lions' den with Daniel. That angel protected Daniel from the lions. When King Darius came to see what had become of Daniel, he was amazed to see that Daniel was still alive, and that the lions hadn't harmed him at all. The king was shocked. The king was so impressed that God had saved Daniel that he made a new law, saying that everyone in the country should believe in and pray to God, because God had saved Daniel from all the hungry lions.

If Daniel had not done what he knew was right, he would have compromised himself. Then no one would have seen the powerful things God can do.

God wants us to be like Daniel. He wants us to do the right thing, no matter what. That's always the best thing to do.

When you have to make a choice between something you know is the right thing to do and something you know would be wrong, compromising will hurt you and others, and it can make you feel really bad about yourself.

If you are in a situation right now where you may be thinking of doing or saying a bad thing, please say this prayer.

PRAYER

Dear God, please help me make the right decision. I may be scared but I trust you, God. You saved Daniel from the hungry lions, and I know you will help guide and protect me too. Amen.

(SAY THESE OUT LOUD)

No one can succeed by doing wrong; true success only comes to people who do the right thing. (Prv 12:3)

If I fear others I will have trouble, but if I trust God and do what is right I will be kept safe. (Prv 29:25)

"Oh no, what if it's too late? What if I already compromised and did something I should not have done?" The good news is, God loves you, child. You need to be honest about what you did, and tell God everything. Tell him you are sorry. If you hurt other people you should apologize to them too. Ask God to give you the courage to make better decisions the next time you are tempted to compromise. You may find this prayer helpful:

PRAYER

Dear God, I am so sorry for doing what is wrong. Please forgive me. Teach me your ways so I won't do this again. Please give me the courage I need to tell the truth and please heal all the people I have hurt. Amen.

Depression

We all feel sad sometimes. Usually we know why we're sad, and our sadness goes away after a while.

But some people feel sad all the time, or often feel sad without knowing why. That kind of sadness is called depression, and it can be a real problem for people who suffer from it.

If you struggle with depression, God has much to say to you. When I was working as a social worker I had many opportunities to work with depressed people. I found that most of them just needed help with their thinking. God has a lot to say to us about our thoughts.

I have been honored to work with all kinds of different people, and what I have learned is that God loves all of us. People who struggle with severe depression may need more than just counseling. I have had the privilege to watch God use many different people and tools and techniques to help heal severe depression. If you are suffering from extreme depression, you should certainly talk to your parents about it, but you should also ask God for help. God knows exactly what you need. In this section I am going to share with you what he has taught me about depression and how it often relates to the way that we think.

The Bible tells us about a man named Elijah, who lived a long time ago. He loved God very much and he felt a very close connection to God. God spoke to Elijah often, but there was a time in Elijah's life when he became very depressed, to the point that he actually prayed that his life would end. This was quite sad, because life is such a precious gift from God, but at the time, Elijah was so depressed that he didn't care about that. What was happening to make Elijah so depressed? Let's find out.

A woman named Jezebel was threatening Elijah's life. She made all kinds of threats against him, and she was basically being a big bully. Elijah became very sad and afraid that Jezebel would have him killed. It also made Elijah sad to know that Jezebel didn't follow God's teachings. Elijah loved God so much, he couldn't understand why everyone didn't love God.

So Elijah ran away. He left his home and started out on a long journey. As he was walking, Elijah became so depressed that he sat down under a tree and prayed to God that he would just die, right there. He actually asked God to take his life away. Can you imagine how sad you would have to be to feel that way?

God then asked Elijah, "What are you doing, and why are you asking me to take your life?" Elijah, feeling very sorry for himself, said to God, "All this bad stuff has been happening to me, plus I am the only one who knows you and loves you."

God knew that He needed to help Elijah with his thinking. God knew that Elijah felt really bad, but what he was feeling bad about was based on what he was thinking. And Elijah's thoughts were all wrong.

God told Elijah to go back home, and God made it very clear to Elijah that there were thousands of people who still loved God.

What came across to me when I read this Bible story is that Elijah really knew God. He prayed to God all the time, and Elijah knew the power of God. One time, Elijah prayed that it would stop raining, and not only did the rain stop, but it didn't rain again for three years! So because everyone needed rain, Elijah prayed that it would rain again, and it did.

So Elijah knew God. He knew that God would answer his prayers, but he still became very afraid and depressed because he was thinking about all the bad things that were happening. This teaches us is that we must be careful what we are thinking about, because the same thing can happen to us. What I mean is that we shouldn't always focus on the bad things in our lives, and that when bad things happen, feeling sorry for ourselves can often end up making us feel even worse. That's when we need to remember that we're not alone, that God loves us, and that God will help us, if we only ask Him.

So getting back to our story, what did God do for Elijah? He not only told Elijah to go back home, but God also gave Elijah some important work to do when he got home. And God corrected Elijah's thinking, by showing Elijah that there were lots of other people in the world who loved God too. All that helped Elijah to stop feeling so depressed.

If you struggle with depression, or feel alone and sad, please say this prayer.

PRAYER

Dear God, I have been feeling alone and very sad lately. I need your help with my thoughts. Jesus, please help me to think better thoughts, and remind me of all the good things and blessings I have in my life. Amen.

Remember, if you always focus on yourself and your problems, they will only get bigger. What you need to do is focus on God. Ask Him to give you a job to do. We all have jobs to do; right now, my job is to write this book. Your job might be to help someone in need. If you do what God asks you to do, you will have peace in your heart and mind. So start thinking about God and how great He is. He'll help you.

(SAY THESE OUT LOUD)

Why are you so sad, my soul? Why so upset inside me? Put your hope in God. I will choose to praise Him and think about all the good things God has done. (Ps 42:5)

I will remember God and I will have hope. (Lam 3:21)

God's great love will help me. He always has compassion on me. (Lam 3:22)

God's blessings are new every morning. (Lam 3:23)

God is faithful and I will wait for Him. (Lam 3:24)

God shows us compassion, and His love never fails. (Lam 3:32)

The Lord is good to those who hope in Him. (Lam 3:25)

Embarrassment

"Oh no, tell me I did not just do that! ... Are they looking at me? What are people going to think of me?"

We have all found ourselves in embarrassing situations. Falling down in public, falling out of chairs, tooting in class. Oh my goodness, are you blushing just thinking about it?

No one likes to feel embarrassed. When all eyes are on us, it can make us become self-conscious. That means that we are thinking about how we look to the people around us.

Why do we react that way? One reason is that we care about what others are going to think of us. We don't like it when people think poorly of us, or when they start laughing at us because we've made a mistake or had some kind of accident.

What should we do in these really uncomfortable situations? Does God even have any words for us in these situations? Yes, He does. Remember, God really does care about

37

what happens to you. He loves us and cares so much about us, that He has actually given us quite a few words about what to do when we feel embarrassed. From those words, we can come up with a plan for what to do when we are embarrassed over something.

Step 1: Ask God for help in the situation. The Bible (Ps 20:1) says, "May the Lord answer you when you are in distress. May the name of God protect you."

Step 2: Assess the situation. If other people are laughing at you, that doesn't always mean that they're trying to hurt your feelings. Maybe the thing that made them laugh--the thing you're embarrassed about--really was kind of funny. At times like that, it's not a bad thing to be able to laugh at yourself too. Perhaps you provided some much needed comic relief in a bad situation. And everyone can have a good laugh, in good fun, without anybody's feelings getting hurt. The Bible tells us that there is a time for everything and a season for every activity under heaven: a time to cry, and a time to laugh; a time to be sad, and a time to dance.(Eccles 3:4) So maybe it's just a good time to laugh. However, if you are not finding anything funny about this particular situation, you may want to store the following words in your heart and mind. That way, the next time you find yourself in an embarrassing situation, you will know what to think about and say.

(SAY THESE OUT LOUD)

Mockers (people who make fun of others) stir up a city, but wise men turn away anger. I am a wise person, and I will not let their laughter make me angry. Prv 29:8

Fear of man will prove to be a snare, but whoever trusts in the Lord is kept safe. I will not fear what other people think of me. I trust You, God, and I know that You will help me. (Prv 29:25)

Every word of God is perfect. God, You are a shield to those who trust in You. I trust in You, God; be my shield. (Prv 30:5)

God opposes the proud, but gives grace to the humble.(Jm 4:6)

Nothing humbles us (makes us feel unimportant or powerless) more than having others see our weaknesses. But God will give you the grace to get through this. It will be OK.

Fear -Feeling Nervous, Scared, Worried or Afraid

Anything that is not of God is fear. Did you know that the statement "Fear not" appears in the Bible 365 times? I once heard someone say that's a "fear not" for every day of the year.

God has a lot to say about fear. He wants you to fear not!

If you are afraid and struggling with fear, God's Word will help you. God will give you strength and courage, but we must go to God and read what He tells us about fear.

In the Bible, the Gospel writer John (1 Jhn 4:18) tells us that there is no fear in love. Perfect love drives out fear. We know God is perfect Love, and the Bible also tells us (Rom 8:38-39) that nothing will ever be able to separate us from the love of God. This is great news! No matter what you have done or failed to do, no matter what you have said, God still loves you and He always will. NOTHING will ever make God stop loving you. If you truly know how much God loves you, you will realize that you don't need to be afraid. God may not like what we do at times, but He never, ever, stops loving us. If you are finding yourself afraid, worried, or nervous, or going through all of the other bad emotions that are linked to fear, please say this prayer.

PRAYER

Dear God, I have nothing to fear. I know you love me and I know you will help me. I trust in you, God. Please help me to stay out of fear. Amen.

No matter what you are afraid of, when you focus on God and say His words out loud, it drives fear away. Because God is love, His words are a weapon that are always to be used against fear. Whenever you feel afraid, ask God for protection and start saying His words out loud. Know that He loves you and is with you. You will find that this really works very well. It is best to memorize some of God's words if you can, so you will always have them with you. Fear will always try to scare you, but God's word will ALWAYS drive fear far away from you. There is power in the word of God, child. Use it and believe what God says.

(SAY THESE OUT LOUD)

The Lord is my light. He saves me; whom shall I fear? The Lord holds my life in His hands; I will not be afraid of anyone. (Ps 27:1)

I turn to the Lord and He answers me. He takes away all my fears.(Ps 34:4)

Whoever listens to God will live in safety without fear of harm. (Prv 1:33)

If you fear people, you will have problems, but if you trust God, He will keep you safe. (Prv 29:25)

Those of you who have fearful hearts, be strong and do not fear. God will come and He will save you. (Is 35:4)

Do not fear, for I am with you. Do not be troubled; I am your God. (Is 41:10)

I am God; I hold your right hand. Do not fear, for I will help you. (Is 41:13)

Do not be afraid of what people will do or say to you. I am your maker and I will comfort you. (Is 51:12-13)

Forgiveness and Boundaries

Jesus told us that we should forgive other people. But what does it mean to forgive, and why do we have to do it?

Because we are all human, none of us is perfect. We have all hurt someone at some point in our life. We all make mistakes and we sometimes do and say things we should not do, and oftentimes that ends up hurting others, even people we love and care about very much.

And sometimes we're the ones who get hurt, when other people do things they shouldn't. When this happens, we have a choice to make: we can either stay angry about what the person did to us, or we can choose to forgive them. Forgiving is sometimes hard to do, especially when we feel like we have done nothing wrong to deserve being treated so badly. When we forgive people, though, we are doing a good thing for ourselves as well as for the people who hurt us.

When we forgive, we are letting go of all of the bad feelings and thoughts we are having. We are letting God take them from us, so we can get that good feeling of peace back in our hearts.

How do we forgive? When someone hurts us, Jesus tells us to pray for that person. The truth is, the person who hurt you is probably hurting too. When people hurt those around them, it's usually because they themselves are struggling with some bad feelings. Having bad and angry thoughts about the person does not help you or the person who hurt you. When you go to God and pray for that person, you invite God into the situation to help you with your bad feelings, and to help the person who hurt you. That is pretty important, because instead of bad feelings everywhere, now you are asking for feelings of peace and love, both for you and the person who hurt you.

That may not feel natural, I know. It can be very hard to do, but Jesus tells us it's the only way we will get our peace back. I don't know about you, but I enjoy good feelings rather than bad ones, so that is why it is important we do this God's way.

BOUNDARIES

Now I want to talk to you about boundaries, because forgiveness and boundaries go together. Sometimes when we forgive people, our relationships with them become even better, because some people repent. That means they have realized what they have done wrong, and changed their ways, so they will no longer hurt you. It is wonderful when this happens, but it doesn't always work that way. Just because we have forgiven someone doesn't mean that they are going to repent or stop acting in a hurtful way.

You should always forgive people who have hurt you, but that does not mean that you should allow someone to continue to hurt you. As I was thinking about this part of the book, God gave me some insights into what He wanted me to say, so I will start with the first thing He brought to my mind.

The Bible tells us in the Gospel of Luke (4:28-30) that one day Jesus was teaching the people who wanted to listen to Him. Even though He hadn't done anything wrong, some people didn't like what He was saying and had become very angry with Him. They chased Jesus out of town. They were so angry and upset they wanted to throw Jesus over a cliff, but Jesus just walked away from them.

Another story comes from the Gospel of John (Jhn 10:39). Again Jesus was teaching the people, and some of them got angry again and tried to grab Jesus to hurt Him, but He escaped their grasp.

So now we have two times that Jesus had to get away from people who were trying to hurt Him. If we take a look at the First Book of Samuel (1 Sam 20:12-13), we find a similar story about a man named David.

There was a king named Saul, but God had someone else in mind to be king. God chose a boy named David. David was a good man, and he loved God. However, King Saul was very jealous of David, and he did not want David to be king. David's best friend was Saul's son Jonathan. When Jonathan went to talk to his dad about David, he found out that Saul was planning to kill David! Jonathan told David about it, so that David would have a chance to leave town and save his life.

You may be wondering, how does all of this tie in with forgiveness? Well, there are people in our world who try to hurt others, and sometimes they may do some bad things to us. If this happens, we should always pray for the person who is doing these things. However, we should not stay in any situation where the person continues to hurt us.

Another way of saying that is that we should create a boundary between us and the other person. A boundary is a kind of border, or space, between two people or objects. For example, if you have a fence around the back yard of your home, that fence creates a boundary between your yard and your neighbor's yard. So if you put some distance between yourself and someone who is hurting you, you are creating a boundary between the two of you.

Some people think that forgiving means staying with someone who is hurting you over and over again. Jesus did not do that, and neither did David. God had good plans for both Jesus and David, and He has a good plan for you too, but just as Jesus and David had to walk away from people who were trying to hurt them, you may have to walk away as well.

We can always pray for people from a safe distance. We can always forgive them in our own hearts, but it does not mean that you should stay in a bad situation. Just because you may need to get out of a relationship or end a friendship does not mean that you cannot forgive the other person. All it means is that you need to put some space between you and the person who has been hurting you. When you do this, the other person may realize what they have done and it might lead them to repent—to be sorry and change their ways. It does not always happen that way, but sometimes it does.

In the Bible (Titus 3:10), we are told that when someone is doing something wrong to us, we should tell that person, once. Please know, child, that if someone is hurting you, it is wrong. If they do it again, we are told to warn them again, and ask them to stop. If they do not change, we are to walk away from them.

It is never God's wish for you to be hurt or abused. He loves you, and if someone is hurting you, you should pray to God. Ask for healing for the person who is causing the hurt, and for yourself as well. Second, if the person does not change, and won't stop hurting you, then you may leave the situation. It's OK. Jesus did it and so did David. I'm sure there have been many others as well.

Let me say another thing about what to do when someone hurts us. Sometimes people hurt our feelings, and sometimes they hurt our bodies. When they hurt our bodies (for example, by hitting us), we say that they have hurt or abused us physically. If someone has physically hurt you or touched you in a way you know is wrong, you need to tell an adult whom you trust about what happened, so they can help protect you from it happening again.

When someone has hurt you, you should pray to God for that person and for yourself, but don't just let it continue to happen. You should get help if your situation is bad. You are not doing anything wrong to tell someone. I will have more to say about this in the "Secrets" section of this book. For now, all you need to know is to tell an adult if someone has physically hurt you, or if they have been doing anything hurtful toward you over and over.

PRAYER for forgiveness:

Dear God, please forgive [name of person] for hurting me. I know I have done some bad things in my life and that I have hurt others too. I am sorry for that. Please fill us both with your peace and love so that we may both stop hurting on the inside. Amen.

The key to forgiveness is to say this prayer over and over again. What I mean by that is, whenever you start thinking about what the other person did to you, and you start feeling upset, you need to pray for them. Don't feed the anger; stop it in its tracks. Say prayers of forgiveness as many times as you need to. I know it might be hard, but when you do this, you really are doing a good thing for both yourself and the other person.

God bless you child, and may His love and peace guide you always.

(SAY THESE OUT LOUD)

Above all, show love to others, since love covers a multitude of sins. I will show love by praying for those who hurt me. (1 Pet 4:8)

Bear with one another, and if someone has a complaint against someone else, forgive each other; because the Lord has forgiven us, so we must also forgive. (Col 3:13)

If I judge not, I will not be judged; if I condemn not, I will not be condemned; if I forgive, I will be forgiven. (Luke 6:37)

Love your neighbor as yourself. Love does no harm to a neighbor (Mark 12:31)

Guilt

Have you ever felt guilty about something? Guilt is that feeling we get when we know that we have done something wrong, or caused a problem, or hurt someone, and we feel really bad about it.

Even though it doesn't feel good, though, guilt can be good as well as bad. It can be good if it leads us to repentance. What does that mean? Repentance means that you feel bad about something you have said or done, and you tell God that you are sorry. Sometimes when we feel guilty, then, that is actually a good thing, because it lets us know that we have done something wrong that caused us to lose the feeling of peace in our hearts, and that we need to repent and ask for forgiveness.

When this happens to us, the best thing to do is to admit our wrongdoing and say that we are sorry to the people we have hurt, and to apologize to God. Once you do this, that feeling of peace should come back. But what if it doesn't? What if you told God what you did and that you really are sorry you did it, and you still feel guilty? That kind of guilt can be bad.

If you are feeling this way, you need to take a look at the thoughts you are having and turn your thinking back toward God. The reason why is that once you say you are sorry and you really do mean it, God forgives you. Remember, He loves you and wants you to have peace in your heart, not guilt. Let's take a look at what God says about this.

The Bible (Heb 4:15) tells us that Jesus understands us. He understands all of our mistakes and He understands how we feel.

The apostle Paul (Phil 3:12-13) had a lot to feel guilty about. He had done a lot of bad things—he'd been a really mean bully to God's people--but then he changed his ways. Jesus helped Paul, and Paul turned into a really good man, but every now and then Paul would think about the bad things he had done, and he would feel bad again. But what Paul learned is that he needed to let go of what happened in the past, and to look forward to the good plans God had for him.

If we spend too much time feeling guilty about the things we have said and done, we will miss the blessings and good things God has for us right now. God does not want you to feel guilty, because He loves you and He will forgive you. All you have to do is ask. Once you tell God you are sorry, start thinking about all the good things God has helped you with. It's important to remember the love He has for you. Knowing that God loves you helps you get peace on the inside, so you can move forward to help other people too.

In the same way, if we are always focusing on ourselves-feeling guilty can cause you to do that—we often won't be aware of how other people around us are feeling. Let's say you have a friend, and that friend is feeling really sad, but you are so busy feeling guilty about something, you don't even notice that your friend needs help.

If instead you would have said, "God, I know you love me, and I am OK because you love me. I am not going to feel guilty today because I know that you have forgiven me," then you would have experienced peace on the inside and you would have been able to help your friend too.

It matters what we think and feel. Sometimes we must adjust our thinking, to get that feeling of peace that Jesus wants us to have. We do this by speaking God's words. And to find the right words, we need to know what God says to us about guilt and peace. Thinking God's thoughts and saying God's words about love and peace will help you on the inside, and it also helps everyone else all around you.

If you happen to be feeling guilty, tell God what it is you have done. Apologize to Him and the people you have hurt, and then pray to God. Here is a simple prayer you may wish to use.

PRAYER

Dear God, I have done something I feel really guilty about. [Say what you have done.] I feel very bad, Jesus, and I am so sorry that I have done this. Please forgive me and please heal the people I have hurt. Forgive me, Lord. Amen.

Now it's time to stop feeling guilty and get your thinking centered on God.
   (SAY THESE OUT LOUD)

Jesus knows my weaknesses and all my mistakes. Jesus understands me and I am OK. (Heb 4:15)

I will not feel guilty about my past; instead I will focus on all the good things God is doing for me.(Phil 3:12-13)

God has plans to help me, not to harm me. I will not spend one more minute feeling guilty and missing what God has in store for me. (Jer 29:11)

God loves me unconditionally. (Jer 31:3)

Jealousy

Have you ever wanted something that someone else had? Did you start feeling upset because they had what you wanted and you didn't have it? That is called jealousy. Jealousy is a very dangerous emotion. If you struggle with jealousy, please read on because jealousy is one of the ugliest emotions you can have. It can really hurt you and those around you. In fact, when you are jealous you are actually creating a problem between yourself and God.

Pastor Josh from Elim Gospel Church in Lima, New York gave a great talk about this topic. I'd like to share with you what I learned from him and what the Bible says about jealousy.

Sometimes you may hear the word envy. Envy is what we call it when you are very jealous, so jealous that you might even hurt someone to get what you want. It is an extreme form of jealousy. But whether you are a little bit jealous or struggling with envy, please read on.

God has a lot to say about jealous feelings and what you can do about them. In the Bible it says that envy (extreme jealousy) "rots the bones." That means that envy is like a poison that makes you feel rotten on the inside. YUCK!

The Bible (Jm 3:16) also tells us that where you have envy you have every kind of evil. Evil means something wicked, or morally bad. It brings harm to anyone it affects.

If you continue to have feelings of jealousy or envy, you actually invite evil into your life. This is very harmful and it can create deep resentment towards people. "Resentment" means bad feelings or even hate towards someone, and it makes you want to be mean to that person. That's why jealousy is so bad, it leads to all those other bad thoughts and feelings toward other people. If you don't stop it, jealousy will end up making you rotten inside. It is really, really bad. That's why James said that wherever you find jealousy, you will find evil too.

Is it wrong to want things, then? No, it is not wrong just to want something. What is wrong is wanting something that belongs to somebody else, so much that you wish it was yours, and not theirs. That's where the real problem starts.

How does this become such a problem? Let me tell you a story. This book actually came about because of something that happened with my daughter. One day I was at home playing the piano, and my daughter became very upset. When I asked her what she was so upset about, she told me that she was jealous of me because I was a better piano player than she was.

I knew that I needed to help her understand that those kinds of feelings would lead to really bad things in her life if she did not get a handle on them and learn what to do about them.

See, the problem with jealousy is that it makes you so focused on what someone else has that you can't see, or you forget what God has done for you. It also causes you to get angry, and that doesn't feel good. Angry at who? Most people don't realize it, but when they get angry because of jealousy, they are really angry at God. Their attitude is, why does God let that other person have the thing that I want, and not me?

When people are jealous, then, they feel as if God owes them something, but what they don't realize, or what they forget, is that God loves all of us. He has given each of us a unique set of gifts and talents. When we are so busy feeling upset about what someone else has, we can't see all the things that God has blessed us with.

This truly is a problem between us and God because very often, the things that you are the most jealous about--the things you want the most, that someone else has--are things that the other person can't just give to you. They can't give you their talents, or their ability, or trade places with you. For example, I could not give my daughter my ability to play the piano. I developed that ability through years of practice and taking lessons. I can't simply give her my abilities. No one can do that.

It's beginning to sound as if, when we're jealous, no one can help us with our bad feelings. So what should we do?

For starters, you must be willing to recognize this truth: that what belongs to others, belongs to them, and not you. You must also be willing to apologize to God and ask Him to help you get rid of these jealous feelings.

But there's more to it than just trying to make yourself stop feeling jealous. Be willing to look at what gifts God has given you. Don't think you don't have any, because you do.

God gives everyone talents and abilities to share. We need to figure out what those are, and concentrate on them. As I explained to my daughter, for example, she can learn to play the piano herself, and if she studies and practices enough, she can become a very good pianist someday. Who knows, she may become better than I am! Or she may decide that her interests and her talents are really in some other area—art, or dancing, or writing, or sports—whatever. The point is, she needs to discover for herself what gifts God has given to her, instead of feeling jealous about the talents that God has given to other people.

You need to find your talents, too, and realize how much God has already blessed you. But sometimes discovering our abilities, and developing them, can take a while, and if you have been feeling jealous for a long time, we need to address that now, so we can get that evil out of your life. The first step is to admit that we have this ugly sin, and ask God to forgive us and help us get rid of it.

PRAYER

Jesus, I have been jealous. I have had bad thoughts and feelings about [name of person and the situation--tell Jesus all about it]. I ask You to forgive me for this sin, and help me to see the good plans You have for me instead of focusing on jealous feelings. This I pray in Your name. Amen.

The next step is to ask God to bless the person you have been jealous of. I know this probably sounds strange and it may feel even stranger, but do it anyway.

(SAY THIS PRAYER OUT LOUD):

Jesus, please bless [name of person]. Thank You so much for all of the gifts that You have given to him/her. I pray that You will bless him/her even more. Thank You and Amen.

I know that may not feel very good right now, but it is what God tells us to do. By doing this you are letting go of all your bad feelings and you are giving them to Jesus, so that He can take them all away from you.

Remember that Jesus is God's Son, and His goal for you is to have a feeling of peace. When you are jealous, you have a lot of evil inside you, and no peace at all.

Jesus also tells us to pray for our enemies and to bless those who hurt us. Now I know you are probably thinking, "But the person I'm jealous of is not my enemy." But to tell you the truth, you have made that person into your enemy. Or maybe a better way to say it is that you have made yourself their enemy. How? By having such bad thoughts and feelings towards them. This is why it is so important to handle this God's way. Although it may be hard to do, it is the only way to restore your peace.

Now if you have already hurt the person you have been jealous of, either by your words or your actions, you must apologize to them. We should always say we are sorry to the people we have hurt.

It is so important for you to know how much God loves you. He has such a good plan for your life, and He has given you so many unique talents and abilities. No one else in the world has the exact same talents and abilities that you do. All you have to do is go to God, and ask Him to show you what He wants you to do. Believe me child, when you are doing what God wants you to do, there will be no time for jealous feelings to come in. If they do, though, turn back to this section and stop those jealous feelings God's way. It's the only way to get your inner peace back, and to get you back on track toward following the wonderful plan that God has for you.

(SAY THESE OUT LOUD)

We all have different gifts. We are to recognize our gifts and use them. (Rom 12:6-8)

Every good and perfect gift comes from God. (Jm 1:17)

Each of us has received a gift to serve one another; use it. (1 Pet 4:10)

We all have different gifts, but the same Spirit; our gifts have been given to us so that we can do good in our world. (1 Cor 12:4)

Loneliness

There aren't many worse feelings you can have than the feeling of being all alone. The feeling that no one cares, no one understands you, and the feeling that you are unloved.

This is truly one of the worst feelings in the world, but do you know it's not true? Yes, I know that you may really be feeling this way, or you may have felt that way at some point in your life, but those feelings are lying to you—they are false.

The truth is that God is our creator, the one who made the entire universe, and He loves you so much, and cares so much about you, that He sent His Son, Jesus, to the earth to live among us, and to teach us how to live. Jesus actually died and came back to life so that we could live with God forever and never, ever be lonely. (See Jhn 3:16.) God also gives His Spirit to everyone who asks, including you! That's how much God loves you.

God's Holy Spirit wants to live with you, and help you every day of your life. God never wants to be apart from you. He loves you so much; He never wants you to feel alone.

When we feel lonely, the real problem we have is with our thinking. We think we are alone, and we think we are un-loved, but those thoughts are simply not true. How do we know they aren't true? Because God is perfect, and God does not lie. God tells us that he loves us, unconditionally—that means no matter what happens, or what we do, God still loves us just as much. So we're never truly unloved. God loves us, always.

So why do we sometimes feel alone? Well, many people don't understand that even though God always loves us, for us to really know and feel God's love, we need to invite God into our hearts and lives. God loves you so much that He never wants to do anything you don't want Him to do, so He patiently waits to be invited into your life.

How do we invite God in? By asking God's Son Jesus into our hearts and lives, because Jesus is the one who will send you the Holy Spirit. The Holy Spirit is a personal helper that will live inside you. The Spirit won't change your personality, or who you are—God made you and He loves you just the way you are—but His Spirit helps you to know and under-stand God's ways. His Spirit will also help you to make better decisions and comfort you. God's Spirit makes it possible for us to live with God forever, because His Spirit lives forever.

So we are never really alone. And remember, Jesus died and came back to life for us to make all of this possible. I know it may be hard to understand, but all God asks us to do is believe in His Son Jesus and invite Him into our lives. He wants to be with you forever, but He needs an invitation. God loves you and He wants to be with you all the time, but He needs to know that you want Him too.

If you are ready to invite God into your life, say this prayer.

Dear Jesus, I believe you are God's Son. Please forgive me for all the bad things I have done. I know that I need you and I invite you into my heart and my life. Please come live with me forever, and please give me your Holy Spirit so that I may never be alone. Teach me your ways, Lord. I want to be with you forever. Amen.

God has a lot to say about how much He loves you. Let's take a look at some of God's words on that subject.

Jesus tells us (Jhn 16:7) that He will send us the Holy Spirit, to be with us always. He did that because He loves us. Jesus also tells us not to be afraid. We are cared for so much by God—He even knows how many hairs you have on your head. (Matt 10:30) That's amazing!

Jesus says, "I am always with you, to the very end of time." (Matt 28:20) This does not sound to me like we are ever alone! And remember, Jesus does not lie. So you can believe Him when He says that God is always with you.

(SAY THESE OUT LOUD)

I am with you and will watch over you wherever you go. (Gen 28:15)

Be strong and of good courage. Do not be afraid, for God is with you wherever you go. (Josh 1:9)

Dear child, if you are feeling lonely, I encourage you to study these words from the Bible. They are God's very own words to us. He is with you always, and He knows what you are going through. He cares so much about you. You must believe this and remind yourself of the love that God has for you. When you are ready you may also want to invite Jesus into your life if you haven't already, and ask Him to give you the Holy Spirit. The Bible calls the Spirit "the Comforter" because the Holy Spirit will give you comfort when you need it. The Spirit will also help you remember the teachings of Jesus. Through the working of the Holy Spirit, peace will come to you, and you will be able to focus on God and the people around you, instead of just sitting there feeling lonely.

Remember, you are not the only person who feels lonely, and oftentimes in these situations, it is very helpful to be a friend to someone else who is in need. You will be doing good for someone else, and you will get a feeling of peace and love in your own heart, because you will be walking with God. You will not feel lonely anymore.

May the Holy Spirit be with you and may you know how much God really does love you. May He walk by your side for all time and may you be blessed as you live out God's great plan for your life. Amen.

Remember child you are never alone!

Lying

"Honesty is always the best policy." I've heard that saying many times, and I have come to agree with it wholeheartedly. Honesty means telling the truth, and not telling lies. We have all told lies at one time or another. A lie is something we say that is not true. For example, if you accidentally broke one of your mom's good dishes, but you tell her that you didn't do it, that's a lie. (There are other kinds of lies, too--for more about that, read the part about "Bad Feelings Toward Other People" (pp.17).

Jesus tells us that the truth will set us free. (Jhn 8:32) Telling the truth also helps us to have peace in our hearts. Lies, though, create all kinds of problems.

One big problem with lies is that once you tell one lie, you have to keep on telling them to cover up the first lie. The more lies you tell, the more lies you have to keep on telling. This can be very exhausting because if you say something that doesn't fit one of your lies, you will have to think up a whole new lie, and it starts all over again. And of course, all this time, you will be worried that someone may find out the truth, and then everyone will know that you have been lying.

None of these emotions are peaceful. Worry and fear create even more worry and fear; they will never create peace. That is why Jesus wants us to tell the truth, right from the very beginning. Don't lie, because lies hurt you and they hurt other people too. They always take your peace away.

Here is a prayer you can say if you are having trouble telling the truth.

PRAYER

Dear God, I want to be truthful and honest all the time. I don't want to lie to others and I don't want to lie to you either. Please help me tell the truth all of the time. Amen.

(Say this out loud)

Telling the truth will set me free so I can have peace in my heart. (Jhn 8:32)

Obeying God

To obey means to follow commands or guidance. When we obey, we say we are showing obedience, or being obedient.

Maybe sometimes you really want to go somewhere and do something, and your parents say no, you can't go. That really stinks, doesn't it? Sometimes you just want to do what you want to do, but you can't.

Think of some of the people that you have to obey in your life--your parents, your teachers, maybe your coach, or, if you're old enough to have a job, your boss. But there's somebody else you should obey too, and that's God. In fact, obeying God is the most important obedience you can ever have in your life.

I used to have a really bad problem with obedience, and I found myself in trouble more than a few times. But once I asked God to give me His Holy Spirit, He started training me in obedience. I'd like to share some of what He has taught me about that subject.

The first thing for you to know is how much God loves you. If He ever tells you not to do something, you can be sure that it is for your own good, and possibly someone else's as well.

As I said, there have been times when I really wanted things my way, and God dealt with me about this. It started one day when I sent my daughter to a full day of classes. This was unusual because we home school, but she had just started participating in a weekly program for homeschoolers.

Anyway, a whole day of classes away from home was new to both of us. I dropped her off in the morning, but around 2:00 that afternoon, I suddenly realized that I had forgotten to pack her a lunch! I felt really bad about it. I couldn't believe that I had sent her off all day with no food and without her water bottle.

A few months later, as I was reading my Bible, I happened to remember that day, and how I had sent my daughter off to class with no lunch. I actually started laughing about it, not because it was funny to think of her not having anything to eat all day, but because I just couldn't believe that I could've done such a dumb thing. I said, "God, I can't believe I did that to her."

At that very moment, God spoke to me!

He said, "This is why it is so important that you obey me, Julie. You can look back on that day and laugh at what you did, because it is not a way of life for you. I want you to think about all of my children in the world whose parents really don't care if their children eat." I said, "Lord, I can't imagine that, it makes me sad to think about it." He continued, saying, "When I ask you to obey me it is for all of my children and other mothers who do not know me and who do not know that what they are doing is wrong. When you obey Me, you allow Me to shine through you, so that the people who do not know Me can see Me through you. Obedience is not always just about you. It's about all of My children around you."

This was so profound for me and such an important lesson, because up until that point I thought that God was only telling me what to do, for my sake, and that it didn't really affect anyone but me. I never really understood that my obedience to God was meant to help others as well.

When we obey God, we give other people a chance to transform their lives--to start a new life with God, and begin their own relationship with Him. That's important because they too can ask for the gift of the Holy Spirit, and get their very own personal helper inside their hearts, and have peace in their lives too.

It was amazing to me that God took that one memory that I happened to be thinking about right at that moment, and used it to teach me about obedience.

I listened to what God was saying to me, and I prayed and asked Him to help me want to obey Him. As I turned to His word (the Bible), I learned that when we obey God, we are actually telling God by our actions that we trust Him and believe Him. (Prv 13:13) The Book of Genesis tells us that Abraham believed God, and God called Abraham righteous, meaning that Abraham did what was right, and believed what God told him.

When God tells us to do something, or not to do something, we should listen and obey Him, because by doing so we are letting God know that we hear Him, we trust Him, and we know that He is telling us this for our own good and for the good of others. God really does know the great plan He has for your life. God wants you to live out that plan so others can see it, and maybe they will like it so much that they will ask God to enter their lives too. If you have ignored God and have not been obeying Him, you may find this prayer helpful.

PRAYER

Dear God, please forgive me for not obeying You. I now understand that if You want me to do something, it is for my good and the good of others. Please give me a mind and a heart that wants to obey You. This I pray in Jesus' Name. Amen.

The next step is this. If you know what God wants you to do, go ahead and do it. You need to show God that you are willing to do what He asks. Once you do what He has asked of you, then He will be able to move forward with you, and give you even more instruction.

If you don't do what God wants you to do, you will get stuck where you are. God will not give you more to do until you complete the task that He has already given you.

It's kind of like when your parents tell you, "No dessert until you eat your dinner." It's the same way with God. You must do what He has asked you to do, before you can move on to the next step.

What if you don't know what God wants you to do? Then you need to pray. Ask God to show you the right path to follow and to reveal to you His good plan for you. He will show you, at the right time. Be patient. Just know that God will give you direction. Then it'll be up to you to follow it.

(SAY THESE OUT LOUD)

If I don't listen and obey, I can't move on with God's great plan for my life. (Deut 30:20)

If I do listen and obey, God will reward me and I will have peace, because I will be walking with God. (Prv 13:13)

When People Won't Believe You

It can feel pretty bad when people don't seem to believe what we say. It hurts when they won't listen to us, especially when we try to tell them something important, and we know that we are telling the truth. It can leave us with a feeling of being unloved. What can we do about this? I'd like to share a story with you.

God asked Moses to go to a land called Egypt and to speak to Pharaoh (who was kind of like a king). God wanted Moses to ask Pharaoh to release, or let go, a lot of people who were slaves. A slave is someone who has to work for somebody else, all the time, doesn't get paid for it, and isn't allowed to leave, or quit. God said that Moses should tell Pharaoh that God wanted Pharaoh to let those people go.

"But what if Pharaoh and his helpers don't believe me when I tell them that You want Pharaoh to let the people go? What if they won't listen to me?," Moses asked God.

Now Moses had a valid point. You see, Pharaoh used these slave workers to build all kinds of palaces and other big buildings for him. Pharaoh would never let them go, just like that. But it was important for them to be let go, because Pharaoh and the other Egyptians treated the slaves really badly. The slaves' bosses would beat them, and make them work all day long without any rest.

So Moses didn't think that Pharaoh or any of the other Egyptians would listen to him or believe what he said.

Plus Moses was afraid that he might get nervous and not explain things just right. Moses was scared because God was asking him to do some things that Moses was not very comfortable doing.

God listened to Moses, but then God had some questions of His own. God asked Moses, "Who gave you your mouth? Who gave you speech (your ability to talk)? Who gave you your eyes? Who gave you your ears?" Well, of course, God had given Moses all those things. God made Moses, just as He made us, and everything around us.

Do you know what else God said to Moses? He said, "Don't worry when people won't listen to you, and don't worry when they won't believe you. Why shouldn't you worry? Because I, God, will help you speak, and I will teach you what to say, and I will teach you how to say it and when to say it." So God was going to give Moses a lot of help.

God even told Moses, "You're right, they won't believe you at first and they won't listen to you, but there is a reason, Moses." Do you know what that reason was? It was so that no human could ever take credit for what God was about to do in the land of Egypt. God's plan was to send Moses there because Moses was willing to obey God, and God was going to shine through Moses. Moses was God's instrument-something that God could use--and God was going to show all of the Egyptians, through Moses, just how powerful He really is.

You see, at first Pharaoh refused to let the slaves go; he wouldn't listen to Moses, just as Moses had feared. So God performed many amazing miracles through Moses, so that Pharaoh and the Egyptians would realize that Moses was telling them the truth. Finally, Pharaoh gave in, and let the slaves go free.

If Pharaoh had just listened to Moses right from the start, and said, "Sure, Moses, I'll let the slaves go, " then no one would have realized that God had anything to do with it, and they would not have seen the mighty things that God can do. The Egyptians had to not believe and not listen to Moses, so that God could show them all who He is.

God gave Moses special talents and gifts, then, to show the people in Egypt that Moses really had been sent by God. And even though Moses was a little bit scared, he knew that he could trust God, even when no one believed what he had to say. And God helped Moses, when it seemed as if there was no hope at all.

No matter what is happening to you right now, no matter how bad you feel, God knows what is happening, and He has a good plan for you. Trust God and He will help you.

There is a reason why no one is listening right now, and why people don't believe you even when you tell them the truth, and that reason is that God has something big planned for you and for all of us. All you need to do is ask Him what He wants you to do and then do it, just as Moses did.

PRAYER

Dear God, please help me not to be upset that no one believes me right now. You know the truth, God, and I know You have a great plan for me. Please help me to know what You want me to do and help me obey You. Amen.

(SAY THESE OUT LOUD)

The Lord is strong and He protects me; my heart trusts in Him and He helps me. (Ps 28:7)

I know You, God, and trust You always; help me when I ask. (Ps 9:10)

God has good plans for me, plans to help me and bring good to me, not to harm me. (Jer 29:11)

Rejection

We have all experienced rejection. What is rejection? Rejection means that someone doesn't want to be with you, or talk to you, or be your friend, even though you'd like to be with them, or talk to them, or be their friend.

Rejection can hurt really bad. When we get rejected, we feel unloved and uncared for, and deeply hurt. But the truth is that God loves us very much. I went through a very bad time in my life once when I felt rejected by people who I thought loved me. At the time I was severely hurt, but now I actually thank God for that rejection, because God used it to show me that I was relying too much on other people for love and help, rather than going to Him for those things.

At that time, I felt incredibly rejected, but today I do not believe that my feelings were the truth. Yes, there was a division, or separation, between those people and me. At that time I thought that if they didn't love me and approve of me, surely God must not love or approve of me either. If these people are angry at me, I thought, surely God must be angry at me too. If I am no longer loved by them, then God must hate me.

That was how I thought. That was the worst time in my life. I felt miserable and cried almost every night. But after a while I realized that God had to take all of those people out of my life so that He could help me to get my thinking right. God was showing me that He was still with me even when others weren't, and He helped me through that time. He showed me that I didn't need to look to other people for love and acceptance. Little by little, I started to trust God.

Finally, one morning I woke up to a voice speaking to me. The voice said:

When you know, truly know, God loves you, it won't matter when others don't. And when you know, truly know, God accepts you, it won't matter when others won't.

God was speaking to me, and He was helping me to heal from all the hurt. He was radically changing my views of Him and who He really is. I was *sooo* relieved. I had felt for so long that if I couldn't please others, God wouldn't love me either. I needed to learn that God does not take away His love. God won't do that, because God *is* Love.

There is no separating us from God's love. I needed to understand that, and God needed to show me, when I felt as if no one cared about me, that He was there. He helped me through all my bad feelings, and He started to teach me how wrong my thinking had been.

I knew that God wanted me to read His words in the Bible, so I started studying the Bible all the time. God also led me to several other books that were very helpful to me in understanding my thinking. (There is a list of some of those books in the back of this book).

Since the Lord started to help me with my thoughts, my feelings started to get better too. God has taught me how to think His way and how to use His words to keep my thoughts and feelings focused where they should be: on Him.

If you are feeling rejected I encourage you to say this Prayer to God:

Dear God, I am feeling very hurt and rejected by other people. Please bless them, and help me not to have bad thoughts or feelings toward them in my heart. I pray that You will comfort me and heal me. I love You, God, and I know You love me. Amen.

(SAY THESE OUT LOUD)

Nothing, not death or life or any power at all can ever separate me from Your love, God. You love me all the time, unconditionally. (Rom 8:38)

God is my help and my strength; I will trust in Him. (Ps 28:7)

As the Father has loved Me so have I loved you; stay in My love. (Jhn 15:9)

I am happy to say that the good Lord has restored all of those broken relationships I had with people. Having those relationships repaired has been a huge blessing in my life. However, I also know now that when I have a problem, I should run to God, because He is my helper and counselor, and He teaches me what to do. I love having people in my life, but God has taught me that if they don't love me or accept me, that is still OK, because God does, and He is my best friend.

Dear child, no matter what, make sure you focus on how much God loves you, and say His words out loud. Read His words in your Bible and know the good plan He has for you. His love is neverending. He loves you so much child, take heart and know that He is with you always.

Sadness

We all feel sad sometimes. Sadness can come from many things: the death of a loved one or a pet, or losing anything that we care about. Everyone has felt sad at some point in their life.

Even Jesus got sad sometimes. One time, for example, a good friend of Jesus, named Lazarus, got sick and died. When Jesus came to see Lazarus's family, He saw how sad they all were over Lazarus's death. Jesus Himself became so sad that He began to cry.

Being sad is a very normal emotion. If you have lost someone or something special, you will feel sad for a while. You should expect this, and you should not feel ashamed or embarrassed about it. It takes time to heal from the loss of a loved one, and you can help yourself feel better by focusing on God and His words.

It may help you to know that Jesus knows exactly how you feel. He cares very much about you and your loved ones. Did you know that Jesus has prepared a place for each of us in heaven? Jesus told us that His Father's house (which is heaven) has many rooms, and Jesus said that He was going to prepare a place for us there, so when we die we can be with Jesus forever. God very much cares about us and the ones we love. Trust in Him when you are sad, and He will help you feel better soon.

If you are feeling sad, talk to God, and tell Him all about it. Use His words too--they will help you find peace.

(SAY THESE OUT LOUD)

The Lord is close to all of us who have a broken heart, and He helps us when our spirits are crushed. (Ps 34:18)

I have the Holy Spirit with me forever, and the Spirit will give me comfort. (Jhn 14:16)

I will not be left as an orphan, Jesus will come to me. (Jhn 14:18)

Jesus never lies. He only tells the truth, and these are His promises to us. All we have to do is ask Him for help. He will heal you on the inside. All you have to do is walk with Him child, and listen to all He has to say. You will feel better soon, and have peace in your heart.

God loves you, child. If you find that you have been feeling sad for a very long time, or most of the time, please see the section of this book that talks about depression (pp 33).

Secrets: When to Keep Them – When to Tell

A person you can trust will keep a secret. (Prv 11:13)

We have all heard secrets; maybe you have some now. Secrets are one of those things we learn about when we are very young.

Many secrets are pretty harmless. For instance, maybe you know that your friend Susie likes a boy named Ben, but Susie asks you not to tell anyone, and to keep it a secret. Or maybe you are planning on surprising someone with a special gift or a surprise party, so you need to hide it from them, to keep them from finding out about it.

These kinds of secrets are OK to keep, because no one is getting hurt by them. In fact, the Bible tells us that if you want to be trustworthy (to be someone that other people can trust), you should not tell other people's secrets.

Being trustworthy is a good quality to have. People should be able to come to you and share private things, without you blabbing it all over the place. Being able to keep a secret will help make you a good friend to someone.

So the rule here is that if no one is getting hurt by keeping a secret, then it's usually fine. There are some things that shouldn't be kept secret, however, and that must be told. Let's talk a little about when you shouldn't keep secrets.

SECRETS – TELLING THEM

Some secrets are dangerous to keep. God has a lot to say about keeping secrets and when we need to tell them. If you are keeping a secret that is hurting, or might end up hurting, you or someone else, you need to stop keeping the secret--you need to tell it. Maybe you're afraid to tell it, but God has some words to help you not be scared. He also gives us guidelines about how to stop keeping a secret that is hurting someone.

If you are a child, and someone is trying to make you keep a secret, or if they are saying to you that they'll do something bad to you if you tell the secret, that is a very bad thing for them to do. If something like that happens, you should go to someone you trust and feel safe with, and tell them about it, because God does not like these kinds of secrets. He will help you through this, no matter what that other person has said to try and scare you.

God says, "Do not be afraid of these people, for no secret is really hidden." God sees everything--He knows what is happening, and He will bring it out in the open. (Matt 10:26.)

What this means is that you should not be afraid to tell the secret, because God already knows it.

God also tells us that nothing in all the earth is hidden from His eyes. Everything is uncovered and laid bare before Him. God wants us to tell the truth, because He already sees it anyway. (Heb 4:13)

The Bible tells us that God will bring every hidden thing into the open, whether it is good or bad. (Eccl 12:14) The Bible (Luke 12:2) also says that all secrets will be made known, and that what has been said in the dark will be heard in the daylight. That means that everything will be exposed, and the truth about everything will be made known. There is no hiding from God.

God is very clear with us that if someone is holding a secret over you, or if you know that someone is being harmed or is in danger because of a secret, it is better to tell that secret and bring it out into the open.

If you know about that kind of a secret right now, you should tell the secret right away. Do not wait, because being truthful will help everyone in this situation. God always wants us to tell the truth, because He wants us to love each other, not hurt each other. And if keeping a secret is going to hurt someone, then you shouldn't keep it—you must tell it.

So if you know about somebody or something that is hurting someone, please tell an adult that you trust and feel safe with. No matter what anyone has said to make you keep the secret, God is much bigger and stronger than they are. He is bigger than anyone, and God will protect you. He will also help you tell the truth.

If you have a secret that you know you should tell, but you are scared to tell it, please say this prayer:

Dear Jesus, I have held on to this secret for too long. Please help me tell it. (Tell God what the secret is.) Please guide me to tell the people who can help me, and forgive me for not telling it sooner. Amen.

Another reason why secrets can be bad to keep is that sometimes people want so much to keep something a secret that they may begin to lie, or even to hurt people, to protect the secret. Pretty soon that person will have no peace on the inside at all. They have become a slave to keeping their secret. Remember what Jesus says, "The truth will set you free." Telling the truth is always the right thing to do. It may seem scary sometimes, and you may not know what's going to happen, but when you know that God is with you, it will all be OK.

(SAY THESE OUT LOUD)

God, You are my hiding place. You will protect me from trouble; You will deliver me and surround me. (Ps 32:7)

Dear God, Your love and Your truth always protect me. (Ps 40:1)

Father God, protect me by the power of Your name. Amen. (Jhn 17:11)

Dear child, I encourage you to please tell someone if anyone is hurting you in any way-- by saying that they will do bad things to you, or touching you in a way that you know is wrong, or doing anything that is making you uncomfortable. No one should ever do these things to you. If someone is forcing you to keep a secret, don't do it. Please tell a trusted adult, and please talk to God about this. He will be your help and He will give you the courage to do what is right. By telling this secret--telling the truth--you may be stopping someone from hurting other children too. God will help you, child, and bless you. God truly cares about you. He loves you so much, He will help you. All you have to do is ask Him for help, and then speak up and tell the truth.

May God be with you and give you the strength and courage to do what is right. Amen.

Selfishness

We all want things at times--food, toys, money, friends, love—all sorts of stuff. That's not always a bad thing, but paying attention only to what we want can lead to selfishness. Selfishness means thinking and caring too much about ourselves, and not enough about other people.

There are many ways to be selfish. Not sharing your candy with your friend, for example. Watching the TV program that you want to watch, instead of the show that your little sister wants to watch. Getting gifts from others, but never giving gifts to anyone. Spending money on yourself, but never giving any money to the poor. You can probably think of other examples—maybe from your own life.

The Bible (Gal 5:22) tells us that the fruit of the Spirit is love, joy, peace, patience, kindness, goodness, faithfulness, gentleness, and self-control. That means that when we ask God to give us His Holy Spirit, and we have the Holy Spirit in us, these are the qualities—the good things about us—that God helps us to develop in ourselves. Did you notice that selfishness was not on that list?

Since God is love, and He wants all of us to love each other, there is no room for selfishness. If you're always thinking about yourself, the things that you want, and how things affect you, you will lose your peace.

The Bible (Phil 2:3) also tells us to do nothing out of selfishness. It instructs us to consider others' interests and not just our own. This means that we should make sure other people are doing OK, and see if we can help them instead of just thinking about ourselves all the time.

Do you know that when Jesus came to earth, He came to serve? That means that He didn't come here to be a big, powerful ruler, with lots of people waiting on Him all the time. He came here to serve others. He washed his friends' feet, He fed people, He healed people. He taught people. He always did something good and kind to other people to show them that He loved them.

Even though Jesus was God's Son, He never ordered people around. He didn't say, "I'm your King, come serve me and give me everything I want." Instead Jesus looked around, saw people who were in need, and helped them. And Jesus was God's very own Son-- He could have done anything He chose to do, but He chose to help people. If Jesus put others first and wanted to help others, shouldn't we do the same?

I know this may not seem easy at times. Our natural way of being is to want to take care of ourselves first and to put our wants ahead of others'. God's Spirit, though, is what helps us to live God's way, and God's ways are not our ways, and His thoughts are not our thoughts. What seems good to us, God may not like. That is why it is so important that we read God's word and find out all about what Jesus taught us. If you haven't already, I encourage you to invite the Holy Spirit into your life (see the prayer on page 63). The Holy Spirit helps us to think like God, and the Spirit also teaches us right from wrong, so we can live the way God wants us to.

If we only think about ourselves, we actually end up hurting ourselves. Being selfish will cause us to lose all of our peace, and to have really bad relationships with people. Think about it–would you want to be friends with someone who was always being selfish, and didn't seem to care about you?

In the Letter of James (Jm 3:16), the Bible tells us that where you have selfishness, you find lots of trouble and evil. But wisdom (God's way) comes from heaven, and God's ways are pure, peaceful, loving, kind, honest, and truthful.

The Bible (Jm 4:1) also says that fights and quarrels happen because of selfishness. That's because a lot of fights start when somebody wants something but doesn't have it and can't get it. They can't have what they want, so they fight about it.

James goes on to say that sometimes people ask God for the things that they want, but they do it for selfish reasons. For example, a person might pray to God for money, but only so that they can spend the money on themselves, buying stuff that they want. And when they don't get the money, they get angry at God for not answering their prayers. But the real problem in that situation isn't with God—it's with the person doing the asking, because they were asking out of selfishness.

God is not happy when we think of ourselves only. He still loves us, of course, but He does not always like the things that we do. We need to make sure we are walking with God, and the only way to do that is to ask God for His Holy Spirit. We must invite God into our hearts and lives. He wants you to feel love and peace on the inside, child, and He has taught us how to have it; all we have to do is ask.

God is not mean; He loves all of His children, and He is a rewarder. He has so many great blessings to give to you, but you need to be willing to give up selfishness so that you can receive God's good gifts and share them with others. When you do this you will have peace in your heart and you will be secure, because you are walking with God. He has good plans for you, child.

If you have been acting selfish and not thinking of others or their feelings, God wants to help you change. He has so many blessings to give you, but you must be willing to do things God's way. His way is always better, and you will always have peace and feel good on the inside when you know that you are following God. If you are struggling with selfishness, please say this prayer.

PRAYER

Dear God, please forgive me for only thinking of myself and what I want. Please help me to think of others, and show me how I can help someone else. Amen.

When you start helping others, you will feel much better about yourself. Try this experiment: pick one person every day and do something nice for them. Pretty soon you will find that you aren't thinking only about yourself any longer. You will feel so good about being kind to others that you will realize it's what you really want to do. The best way to feel better about yourself is to help someone else.

(SAY THESE OUT LOUD)

A selfish person is unfriendly. I am not unfriendly; I will think of others and do good to them. (Prv 18:1)

I will do things God's way, and He will bless and reward me. (Prv 28:20)

Stress

Ever feel as if you've got more stuff going on in your life than you can handle? Maybe you're having trouble keeping up with your homework, or your team is playing in a big game this weekend and you don't feel ready. When you have those kinds of feelings, that's stress. Sometimes when we're feeling stress, we say that we're "stressed out."

We have all been stressed out at some point in our lives, but did you know that stress actually comes from not trusting God?

Think about this. If you really trusted God, you would have no reason to be stressed out. Now if you are studying for a big test tomorrow at school, and you're feeling stressed over it, you may be thinking, "God won't take that test for me." Well, you are right, God won't take that test for you, but if you pray and study and do the best you can and still fail, have you thought about whether it may be part of God's plan for you?

Remember, God has a great plan for your life. If you are trying to do something that is not a part of that plan, you may not succeed. And you will find yourself struggling, not because God does not want you to do well, but because He knows there is something better for you, even though you may not realize it yet or see it yet.

Here's an example. When I started college, I went into computer science, mostly because my dad thought that I'd be able to get a good job that way. At the time, I didn't seem to have any better ideas, so I said OK.

Well I failed every class. I hated it and I especially could not stand all the math. I tried and tried, I studied and I prayed, I even got tutors, but I continued to get failing grades. I had no peace and felt frustrated all of the time. Was it because I was stupid? I don't think so.

Looking back on that time, I now see that none of it was God's plan for my life: not math, not computers, none of it. God's plan for my life was to make me a healer and a minister. He knew that I would be happiest if I were serving Him, and boy, was He right. I love what I do now.

None of those computer classes would have helped me to do what God had planned for my life. I needed to give up what I thought was best, so that I could learn what God wanted for me. Now for sure, I had a very long road still ahead of me. You see, back then I didn't know God the way I do now. I didn't realize that I needed to invite Jesus into my heart and my life. And I certainly knew nothing about asking Jesus for the Holy Spirit. So I kept hitting a lot of bumps in the road, and making bad decisions.

At that time in my life, I was not looking to God or asking Him what I should be doing. So I just kept on doing what I was doing, and trying harder and harder. I prayed, but only for what *I* wanted; they were selfish prayers. All I got for it was failure in my classes, my health, and my relationships. School, and everything else, was very hard for me at that time.

Well, as I said, it was a long road that I had to follow, but eventually I came to know God, because He sent a mentor (a kind of teacher) to help me. She taught me how to invite God into my life, and she spent many years training me in God's ways. Today I am much happier than I was back then.

And I can see now that I was never meant to succeed in computer science; that wasn't God's plan for my life. I've also learned that the best thing I can do when I'm feeling stressed is to trust in God, because I know that if I let Him guide me, everything will turn out OK.

I don't want any of you to be as stressed out as I was in college, or feeling as if your life is just one failure after another.

If you are under stress, please say this prayer:

Dear God, I have been stressed out about [name whatever it is]. Please forgive me, Lord. I know you have a good plan for my life; please show me what you want me to do. And help me do it. This I ask in Jesus' name. Amen.

(SAY THESE OUT LOUD)

God, I will trust in You at all times; I will pour my heart out to You. You are my protection and my refuge. (Ps 62:8)

Your words are a lamp to my feet and a light for my path. (Ps 119:105)

In all Your ways acknowledge God, and He will make your paths straight. (Prv 3:6)

Conclusion

I hope that you have found this book helpful. If this book does anything at all, I pray that it will help you to know God and enter into a close relationship with Him. My prayer is that you will invite Jesus into your heart and life. And that you will ask Jesus to fill you up with the Holy Spirit, so that you can have peace; that beautiful peace that Jesus came down to give us.

I am so happy that God has been so patient with me through all my years. I do wonder at times, if only I had known this information sooner, could I have saved myself years of heartache and struggle? Only God knows that, but I love where I am now. And I am very happy to be able to share this information with you, and possibly save you from years of struggling as I did. Ask God what His good plan is for you, because He surely has one.

All the things that God has taught me and continues to teach me make me happier and more peaceful each and every day. It has been one interesting ride! I pray that you will meet God now, and be filled with His love and peace. If there is one thing that I know for sure, it's that only when you are doing what God wants you to do will you be the happiest of all.

Note from the Author:

If you found this book helpful please leave me a message at

Christforkidsministries.com

I'd love to hear from you.

Julie

The Holy Bible

Joyce Meyer, *Battlefield of the Mind for Kids*

Joyce Meyer, *Battlefield of the Mind for Teens*

Joyce Meyer, *Battlefield of the Mind*

Joyce Meyer, *Power Thoughts: 12 Strategies to Win the Battle of the Mind*

Joyce Meyer, *The Secret Power of Speaking God's Word*

Christforkidsministries.com

CPSIA information can be obtained
at www.ICGtesting.com
Printed in the USA
FFOW04n1959211115
18666FF